How to Draw & Paint Animals

by

Helen Webster

ARCTURUS

Arcturus Publishing Ltd
26/27 Bickels Yard
151–153 Bermondsey Street
London SE1 3HA

Published in association with
foulsham
W. Foulsham & Co. Ltd,
The Publishing House, Bennetts Close, Cippenham,
Slough, Berkshire SL1 5AP, England

ISBN 0-572-03012-6

British Library Cataloguing-in-Publication Data: a catalogue record for this
book is available from the British Library

Editor: Rebecca Panayiotou
Text design: Chris Smith
Cover design: Stünkel Studio

Printed in Singapore

contents

introduction

The world of animals offers many exciting subjects for young artists. In the following pages I will be presenting a series of mini art classes to show you how to get the best out of a wide range of materials, from watercolours to acrylics and poster paints.

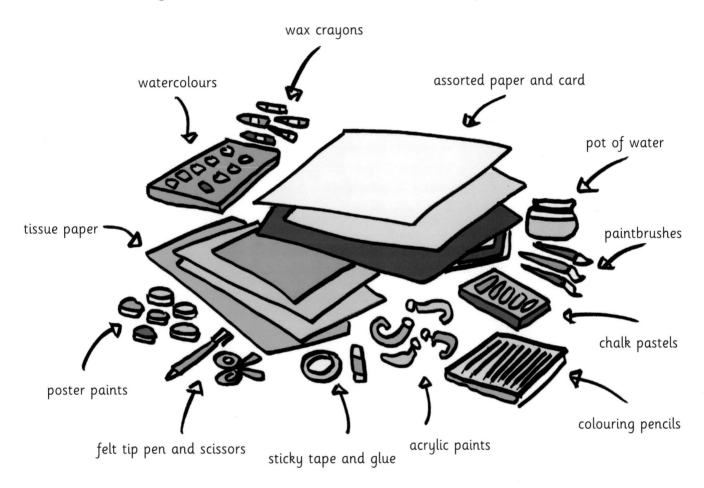

Each double-page spread offers you an opportunity to create a fantastic painting or drawing. As you progress through the book the exercises become slightly harder, ensuring that your skills continue to improve. All you have to do is follow the simple step-by-step guide provided with each project.

The many different ideas presented to you can easily be adapted and changed to suit your needs. The more competent artists among you may want to use them to provide inspiration for their own personal art projects.

However you decide to use the book, have fun – and don't be afraid to experiment. Before you know it you will have a fantastic masterpiece to your name.

how to draw a cat using circles triangles and sausages!

you will need:

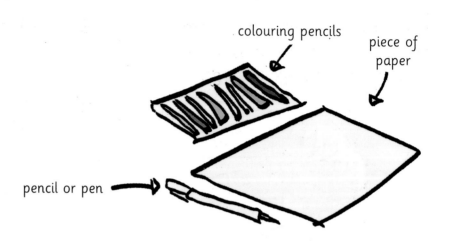

colouring pencils

piece of paper

pencil or pen

Sometimes, when learning how to draw an animal, it's handy to break down the animal's figu into different shapes. So we're going to build up a cat using circles, triangles and sausages.

❶ Draw a circle.

❷ Now draw four small triangles on the circle's edge as shown.

❸ A final triangle, which forms t nose, goes upside down in the centre of the circle.

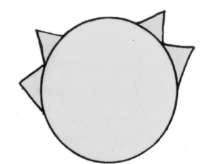

❹ Next draw a large semi-circle for the cat's body.

❺ The feet are also semi-circles – very small ones that have the flat edge facing downwards.

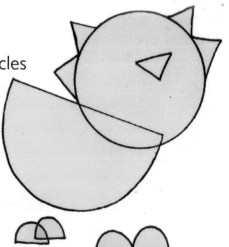

6 Now draw six curved lines for the whiskers and join the body and feet together with sausage-like legs.

7 The tail is also a long curly sausage!

8 To finish off, simply add two circles for the eyes, some raised eyebrows, zig-zags for the ear tufts, a small mouth, and any markings that you want on the fur.

how to draw easy peasy crocodiles

you will need:

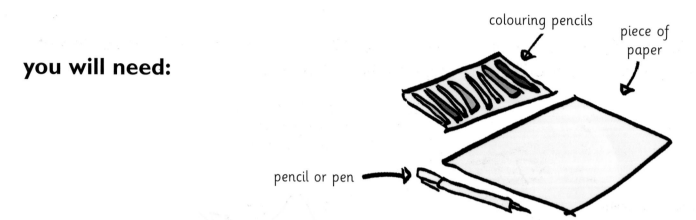

colouring pencils

piece of paper

pencil or pen

You'll impress all of your friends at school when you quickly whip out your pencil and in a quick flash of the wrist draw a cartoon crocodile!

❶ The first stage is to draw two lines that should look like a hair grip, lying on its side.

❷ To form the mouth, simply draw a sideways 'V'.

draw a V on its side

❸ You're now ready to join the mouth to the body and add four sets of little stick legs.

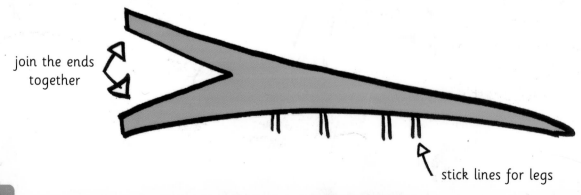

join the ends together

stick lines for legs

4 Now we need lots and lots of little zig-zags! Fill the mouth with teeth and add lots of zig-zags to the crocodile's back, right to the end of his tail.

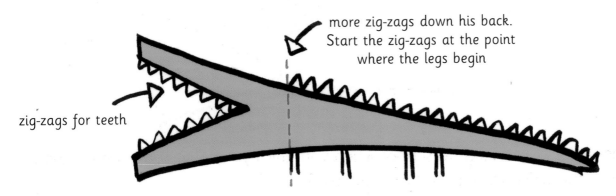

more zig-zags down his back.
Start the zig-zags at the point
where the legs begin

zig-zags for teeth

5 Finally, draw four little sausages at the ends of the legs for the feet and give your croc some eyes. Hey presto! You've made yourself a cartoon crocodile!

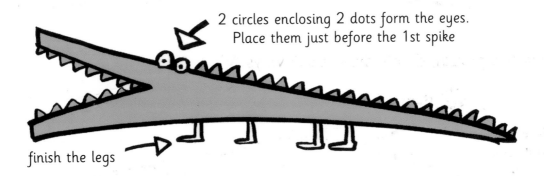

2 circles enclosing 2 dots form the eyes.
Place them just before the 1st spike

finish the legs

Once you've got the hang of it, you'll be able to draw a crocodile from any shaped line. Just remember to follow the five simple steps!

how to draw a cartoon dinosaur

you will need:

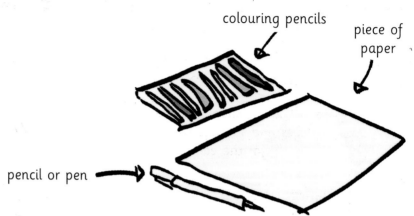

colouring pencils

piece of paper

pencil or pen

We are now going to draw… the dinosaur!

❶ The building blocks of a dinosaur are its body and head, and these are made up of two eggs – or squished circles.

❷ Now join up the two eggs with a curved line and add a curved tail. The tail should be the same length as the head and the body.

curved line

the curved tail is as long as the head and the body

❸ Add two extra lines to complete the dinosaur's neck and tail.

the neck should be thinner at the top and thicker at the bottom

join from the bottom of the body to the end of the tail

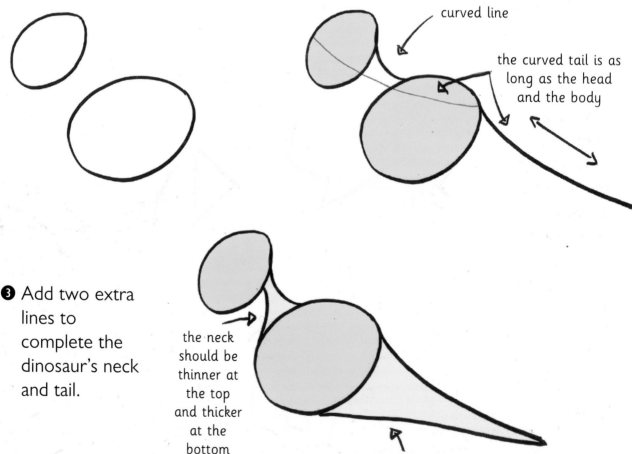

4 The eyes go at the top of the head, in between two small sausage ears. The arms and legs are very simple. Just follow the diagram and it's four easy steps!

5 Now draw a long line of zig-zags, starting at the top of the dinosaur's head and going right down to the bottom of his tail.

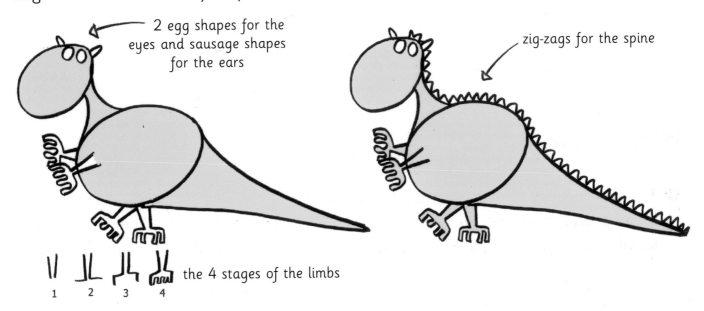

2 egg shapes for the eyes and sausage shapes for the ears

zig-zags for the spine

the 4 stages of the limbs
1 2 3 4

6 If you've drawn the outline in pencil, you can now go over the finished drawing with a pen. Just rub out the pencil marks and, left behind, you have a perfectly drawn dinosaur. Wahoo!

On the next page you can find out how to turn a dinosaur into a dragon!

how to turn a dinosaur into a dragon!

If you can draw a dinosaur then you can draw a dragon. There are four things that you add to a dinosaur to turn it into a dragon:

so you start from this stage (see page 11)

1) *Wings*. These should start at the point where the dinosaur's neck meets its body.

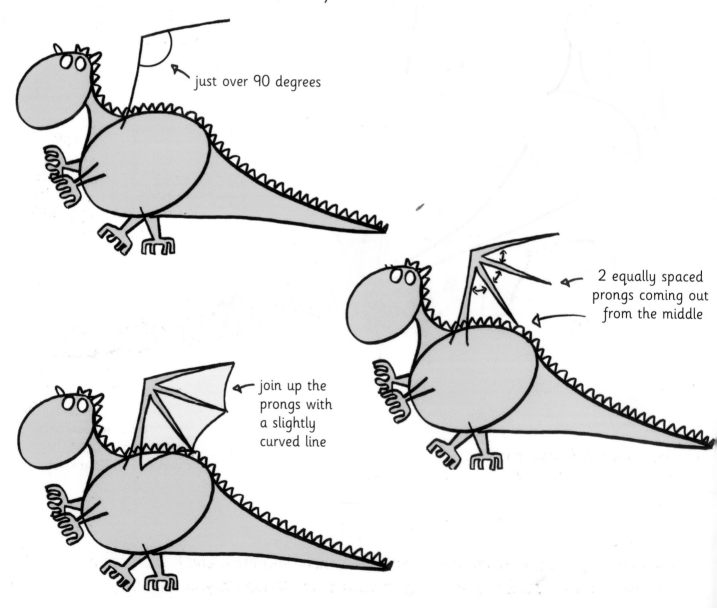

just over 90 degrees

2 equally spaced prongs coming out from the middle

join up the prongs with a slightly curved line

2) *Scales.* A dragon has scaly skin. If you want, you can draw scales all over the body, but I think it looks more effective to draw just a few on the underbelly.

3) *Pointy tail.* Add a triangle to make his tail pointed.

4) *Fiery flames.* Dragons can breathe fire! You have two choices here. You can either give your dinosaur a closed mouth and simply draw some nostrils with smoke wafting from them. Or you can make him look really exciting with his mouth open, teeth sharp and pointy and hot fire spurting everywhere. It's up to you!

to make the dragon breathe fire, draw a triangle in the fat end of his head, add zig-zags for the teeth and wiggly swirls for the flames

to suggest the scales, draw some little 'u's over the belly area

place a triangle at the end of the pointed tail

I think that dragons are much more frightening than dinosaurs, and if a dinosaur and a dragon had to fight, I bet that the dragon would win. What do you think?!

how to create a swirly lizard using felt tip pens

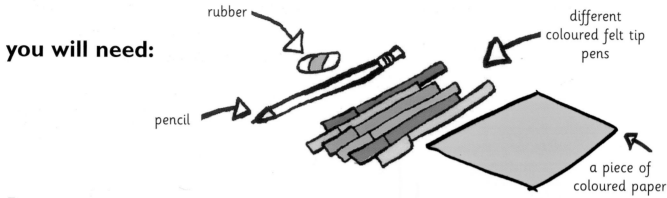

you will need:

rubber

different coloured felt tip pens

pencil

a piece of coloured paper

For my next picture I am going to draw a prehistoric lizard.

❶ Get your piece of paper, pick up a pink felt tip and draw your lizard. The one I've drawn is very similar to the crocodile, except that I've given the lizard a humped back and a curled tail. (If you're not quite sure of the shape you're going to draw, I would draw it in pencil first and then go over it with your felt tips.) Next, use a blue pen to draw some bubbly clouds.

❷ Get your pink felt tip again and colour in the spine on the lizard's back as well as his legs. Now fill the body with lots and lots of little circles. Then, with the same pen, fill every circle with a tiny dot. Use a blue felt tip pen to fill the clouds with lots of spiral 'shells'.

❸ Now use a green felt tip to draw the grass as shown here.

❹ Next pick up an orange felt tip and fill the sky with swirling lines that wrap around the clouds and lizard.

❺ It's time to go back to the lizard. Take your pink felt tip and draw circles around the small circles, and more circles around the bigger circles, until all the space is filled!

And there you have it…a very swirly looking lizard.

What a masterpiece!

you will need:

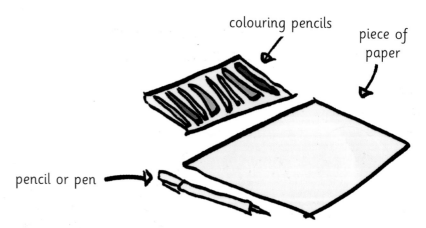

colouring pencils

piece of paper

pencil or pen

An elephant is made up of a rainbow, three boxes, three circles and a banana! Once you've memorised where they go, you can draw an elephant again and again and again.

❶ So let's start with the rainbow arc – the body. This arc should be fairly big and just a little to the left of your page.

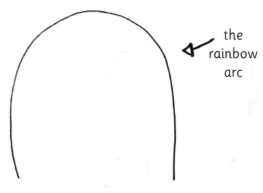

the rainbow arc

❷ Now draw three boxes at the bottom of the arc. When you join them up you can make out where the legs are.

draw 3 boxes to make the legs

❸ The biggest and most important circle is the head. Put this on the right-hand side or, if you want the elephant to look directly at you, in the centre.

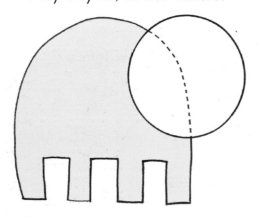

❹ For the ears, place two smaller circles either side of the head.

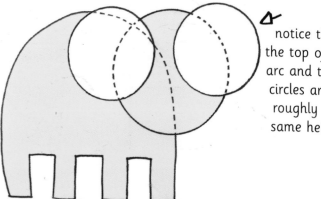

notice that the top of th arc and the circles are a roughly the same height

5 The trunk is easy peasy. Just imagine a long banana with a letter 'V' at the end! Voila!

a single curved
line for the tail

a banana trunk

the letter 'V'

I've used oil pastels, but you can use chalk pastels or paints if you want

a piece of brown envelope paper

you will need:

Now for something completely different — giraffes. These are lovely creatures and ever so simple to draw.

Here's a basic outline for drawing a giraffe.

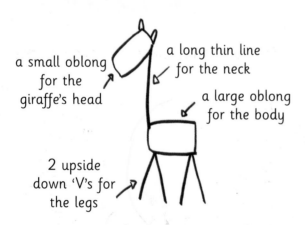

a small oblong for the giraffe's head

a long thin line for the neck

a large oblong for the body

2 upside down 'V's for the legs

❶ Get your envelope paper and draw a big zig-zag across the page. Lightly shade it in with the same colour.

❷ Using a vibrant yellow, draw the basic outline of a large giraffe, and fill it in.

❸ Now add two baby giraffes, following behind.

4 Use the same yellow to draw a big sun in the sky and green to shade around the giraffes to make the grass.

5 Use brown to cover the giraffes' bodies with brown splodgy circles and then shade in the sky with blue.

6 Use the blue to go over the outline of the giraffes, carefully adding details like the tails, the eyes and the ears.

Doesn't it look nice? I think this is my favourite piece of work so far.

how to draw animals using the playdough technique

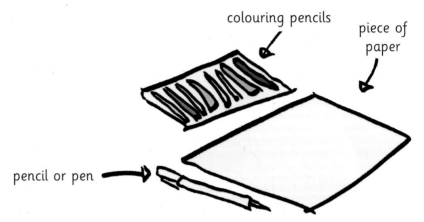

colouring pencils

piece of paper

you will need:

pencil or pen

Another way to draw animals is called the 'playdough technique' and it's very easy. All you have to remember is that every animal starts off as two balls of playdough stuck on top of each other. To demonstrate, I'm going to show you two ways to draw a dog – either standing on two legs, or on all fours. First let's look at a dog standing on two legs:

❶ Draw two 'playdough' balls on top of each other.

❷ Draw two feet at the bottom of your figure. They look like little paddles.

❸ Now add the arms and ears. You'll notice that they are exactly the same shape.

❹ Draw an upside down triangle for a nose and a small pointy tail in between the arm and leg.

❺ It's up to you to add your own fur markings and the expression on the face.

Now let's look at the dog on all fours:

❶ Again, draw your two doughballs, this time side by side.

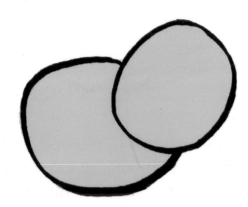

❷ Draw the same two paddles at the bottom of the body.

❸ Add another pair of legs and some ears.

❹ The curved tail goes in the top left-hand corner.

❺ Again, add any final touches and you have yourself a cracking dog!

how to draw a manic monkey

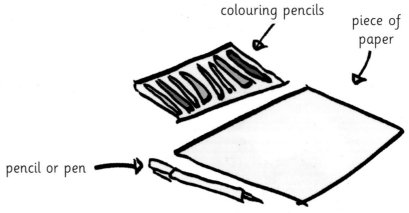

colouring pencils

piece of paper

you will need:

pencil or pen

Now let's try the 'playdough technique' with a monkey!

❶ First draw your two doughballs to form the head and body.

❷ Add the legs.

❸ Now add the arms.

❹ Give your monkey some ears and a tail.

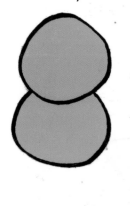

❺ Draw a smaller circle on the monkey's head for a face.

❻ Now simply add the monkey's facial features and colour him in. Very cute!

Follow exactly the same steps to draw a monkey on all fours:

❶ Again, draw your two doughballs.

❷ Add two long, gangly legs.

❸ Add some arms at an angle away from the body.

❹ Draw a curly tail and add the ears either side of his head.

❺ The face is a smaller circle in the centre of the head. Finally, give your monkey a cheesy grin!

how to do animal shortcuts

you will need:

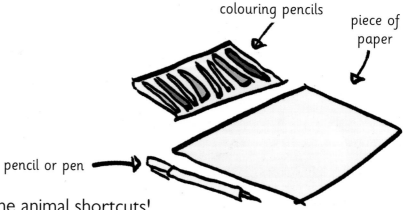

colouring pencils

piece of paper

pencil or pen

Now we're going to look at some animal shortcuts!
Often the only things that distinguish one animal from another are the shape of the nose, the ears and the tail. Notice here how it's not until stage 4 or 5 that they look like different animals! I bet you never realised until now just how much these animals had in common!

❶ ❷ ❸

Will it be a mouse or will it be a rabbit?

❹

big round ears

long ribbed tail

long thin ears

short fluffy tail

①

②

③

④

A pig or a reindeer?

⑤

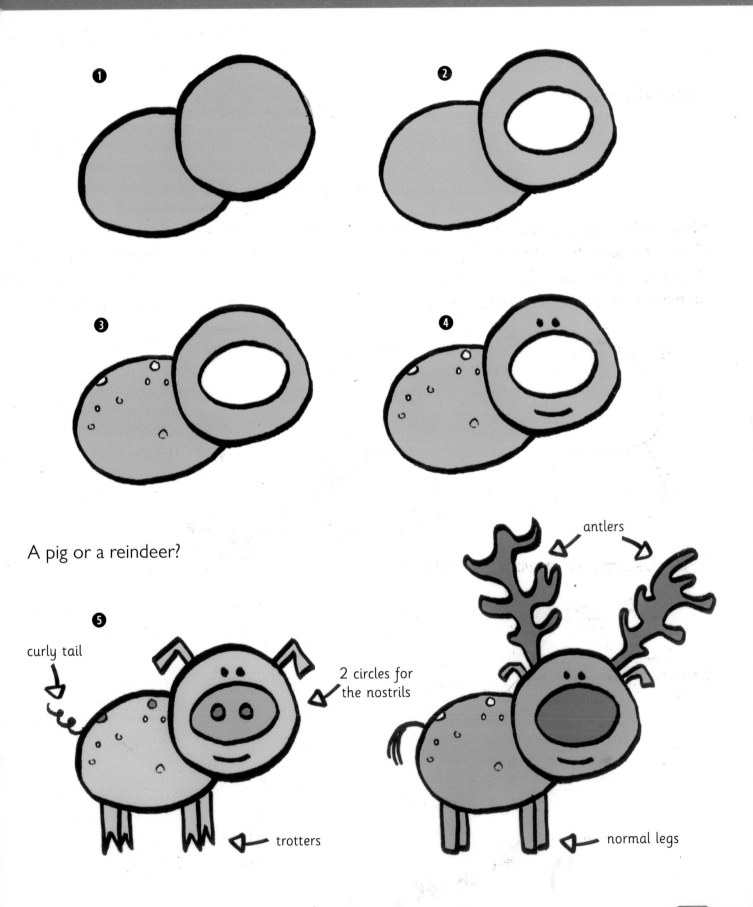

curly tail

antlers

2 circles for
the nostrils

trotters

normal legs

25

you will need:

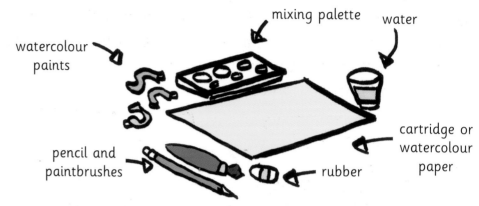

mixing palette

water

watercolour paints

pencil and paintbrushes

rubber

cartridge or watercolour paper

Let's look at watercolour paints. The really good thing about watercolours is the way they mix together when wet – you can create some really cool effects by letting the colours run together.

❶ Get your paper and draw the rough outline of a cat.

❷ Where the different body parts join together, rub out the pencil marks.

❸ Now dip your paintbrush in water and 'paint' the inside of your cat.

❹ Use yellow paint to go over some of the wet paper. Then use some red to paint over the remaining area. You will see the two paints blend together to make lots of gorgeous colours.

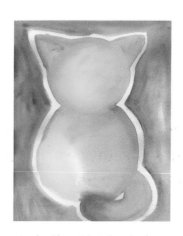

5 'Paint' around the cat with clean water, but leave a space around him so that the colours inside and outside don't mix.

6 Go over the water with some blue paint.

7 Then paint over again with some green and yellow paint.

8 Wait until the paint is completely dry, then finish off by drawing in the face and whiskers. Wonderful!

how to paint a lovely lion with watercolours

you will need:

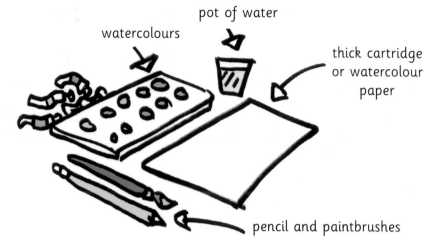

watercolours

pot of water

thick cartridge or watercolour paper

pencil and paintbrushes

Now that we know how to mix watercolours together, we are now going to look at how to layer colours. Keeping with the cat theme, we are going to paint a roaring lion!

❶ Get your piece of paper and do a rough pencil drawing of your lion.

❷ Paint over the whole page with water. Using burnt umber paint (or mix some yellow and brown together) fill in the lion's mane.

❸ When this has dried, add another layer of yellowy-brown paint to the mane and colour the face with a warm yellow.

❹ Wait until the paint has dried before adding another layer to the mane, this time including a bit of orange in your paint mixture. Carefully paint the outline of the mouth and its cavernous contents in brown.

❺ Paint the nose and cheeks a rosy pink and add some pink to the mane. When this is dry add some more brown, yellow and orange. Paint the ears with the same colour you used for the face.

❻ Add more and more colour to the mane, building up its depth and texture. Lastly, fill in the eyes and add a few whiskers. Finished! What a roaring painting!

you will need:

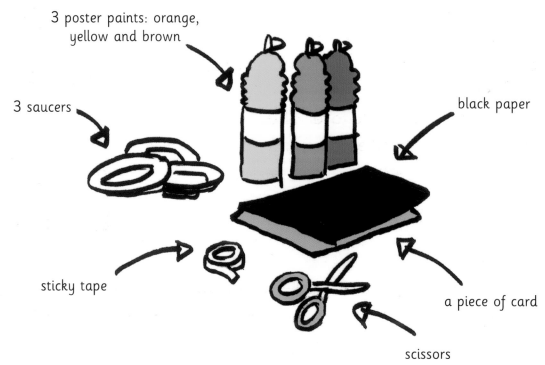

3 poster paints: orange, yellow and brown

3 saucers

black paper

sticky tape

a piece of card

scissors

Right, let's have some fun! For this picture we are going to print with paint. Printing is really cool because you never quite know how the paints are going to stick.

Before we start, we have to make the printing blocks.

a) Get your card and draw three different sized triangles. (You can draw them by hand or use a ruler – it's up to you.) Then cut them out. These triangles are your printing blocks.

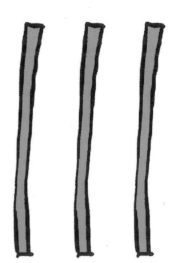

b) Put your triangles to one side. Now cut three strips (about one centimetre/half an inch wide) out of the leftover card. These strips will act as handles for your printing blocks.

c) To make the handles, fold each strip in half. Then bend the ends upwards to make little flaps. Attach a handle to each triangle by sticking down the flaps with sticky tape.

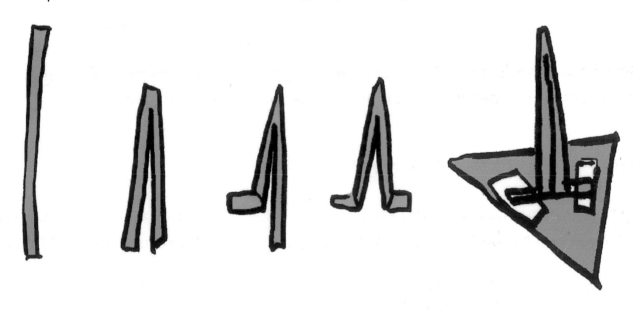

d) Now pour each of your poster paints into a separate saucer, so you have a yellow saucer, an orange saucer and a brown saucer. Great. You're ready to begin!

❶ Dunk your biggest printing block into the orange paint. Now firmly press down in the bottom left-hand corner of your page.

❷ Now get the medium-sized printing block and dunk it in the brown paint. Print in an arc as shown.

❸ Pick up your smallest printing block, dunk it in the yellow saucer and print a smaller arc of triangles beneath the brown triangles.

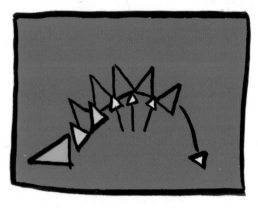

follow this pattern

❹ Pick up the medium-sized block again and dunk it first into the brown saucer, then lightly in the orange. Print a third arc.

❺ Again, dunk the small triangle into the yellow and print another arc.

❻ I finished off with the brown, medium-sized block, but you could go on and on if you want, experimenting with the endless amounts of sizes and effects! To complete the picture, get a black felt tip pen and draw in the hedgehog's eye.

If you don't have a felt tip to hand, just dunk your little finger in the brown saucer and press down where you want the eye to be.

how to paint a toy horse

you will need:

acrylic paints (or any kind of paints you can get hold of)

water

brown envelope paper

paintbrush and pencil

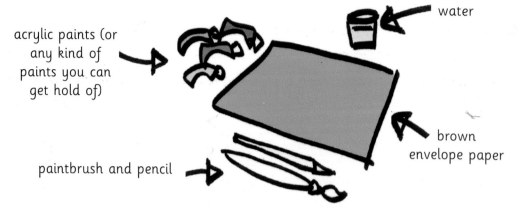

As a child I had a toy horse on wheels that I used to pull around everywhere. I loved it because it looked old and ornate and had a lovely pattern on the wheels and saddle. I'm going to try and recreate that feel of age, pattern and colour in this painting of a toy horse.

❶ Get your brown paper and, using a pencil, draw the outline of your horse.

❷ Get some white paint – not too watered down – and fill in the background.

❸ Now get some light brown paint and paint in the areas of the body that you think would be shaded or dark.

❹ Use thick red paint to neatly fill in the saddle, the centres of the wheels and the ribbon on the tail.

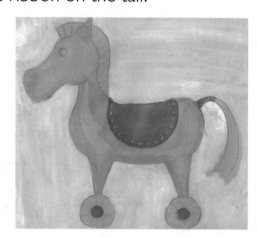

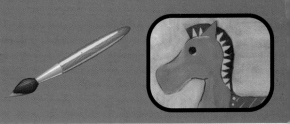

5 Now use your yellow paint to colour the horse's tail, saddle studding and mane. Finish by using the yellow to highlight the lighter areas of the horse's body.

6 Get a dark, thick brown and fill in the rest of the mane and the wheels. If you're brave use a tiny brush to go over the outline of the horse.

7
Finally, get a thick white paint and draw two extra circles on each of the wheels. Then use your yellow to paint a circle of dots between the two white circles.

Finish off by adding some yellow diagonal stripes to the saddle. Wonderful!

how to paint creepy crawlies

you will need:

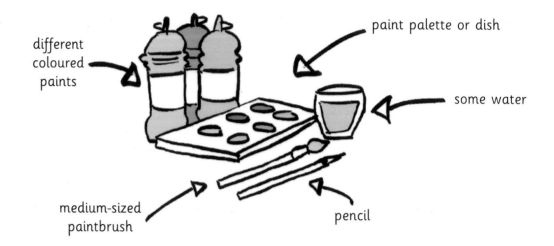

different coloured paints

paint palette or dish

some water

medium-sized paintbrush

pencil

We're going to paint something very simple – the snail! The great thing about the snail is that it can be drawn in about five seconds and it's very easy to do.

❶ Begin with the shell. Start in the middle and draw one long continuous spiralling circle.

❷ Next comes the body. It looks like a pointy sausage.

❸ Finally, we need to add the antennae. These are achieved by drawing a large capital 'V'.

❹ Now that you have drawn the basic shape, you can have lots of fun deciding how to fill in the shell. Here are some examples:

a spotted shell   a striped shell   a colour-filled shell

Once you've mastered the technique, you can use it as the starting point for many other creepy crawlies…

to make a wood louse, take away the shell and add lots of tiny legs to each side of the body

a slug is so easy: just take away the shell from a snail. Ta da!

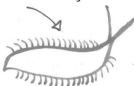

to make a butterfly, don't take away the shell, but add another one to the other side

then add 2 smaller ones at the bottom

how to paint a porky piggy oil paints

you will need:

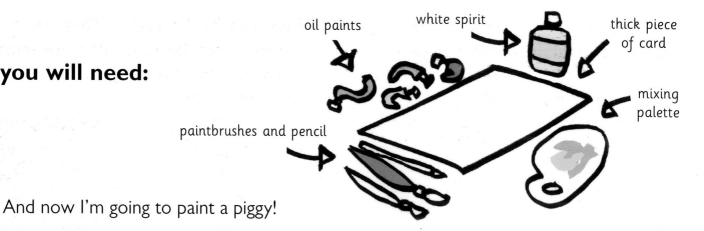

oil paints

white spirit

thick piece of card

mixing palette

paintbrushes and pencil

And now I'm going to paint a piggy!

❶ With a pencil draw a big rosy pig onto a thick piece of paper or card. (For instructions on drawing a pig turn to page 25.)

❷ Paint the background with a large brush. Include as many different shades of green, yellow and blue as you want.

❸ Mix together some orange and pink and use a smaller brush to fill in the body. A bit of yellow will perk his bottom up a bit!

❹ Use pink and orange for your piggy's face.

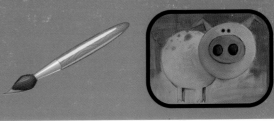

5 Add a bit of brown to your 'body colour' paint and mix until you're happy with the shade. Then paint in the nose and the back pair of legs and trotters.

6 It's time for the nostrils. They are an even darker shade, so add some more brown to the mix and paint in the massive circles.

7 Using the brown on its own, put a small amount on a clean dry brush and dab a few circles on top of the pig's body to give him those big freckles that pigs have. Lastly, use a dark brown

or black to paint in the eyes. Oooh, and I almost forgot, you have to remember to paint in his wonderful corkscrew tail!

how to paint a psychedelic elephant!

you will need:

poster paints, watercolours or acrylics
(whatever you can get hold of!)

glass of water

a piece of
thick paper or
card

a paintbrush and a pencil

I think you're really going to enjoy doing this picture. I definitely did! The good thing about elephants is that they are sooo big. So when painting an elephant you can have lots of fun filling the body and head with weird and wacky colours and markings. You don't have to strictly follow what I've done. Just use your imagination to think of cool and exciting patterns!

❶ First draw your elephant in pencil. (Have a look at page 16 if you need to.)

❷ Now fill the elephant's body with lots of stars.

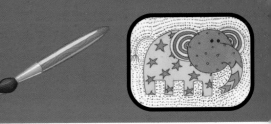

❸ Get your yellow paint and colour in the spaces around the stars.

❹ Clean your paintbrush, cover it in red paint, and colour in the stars.

❺ Now it's time for the ears. I chose to do semi-circles within semi-circles, but you could do whatever you fancy. I drew the pattern with a pencil before I used my paintbrush to paint each alternate semi-circle red.

❻ I decided to cover the elephant's head with lots of tiny circles and fill the trunk with bigger and bigger arrows.

Turn to the next page to see how to finish the psychedelic elephant!

❼ I painted the elephant's head with orange, leaving the little circles clear. After a bit of thought I decided to paint these circles yellow. Last of all, I painted the trunk with alternate colours of orange and yellow.

❽ You could stop here, but it's much more fun to carry on! With a clean brush, get some blue paint and dot your way round the outline of the elephant. Once you've gone the entire way round, do it again!

❾ Now get some lighter blue or green and go around the elephant again and again, changing the colour of paint whenever you want, until you have filled the page with colourful dots. Then get a black pen, or put some black paint on your brush, and go round the outline of the elephant.

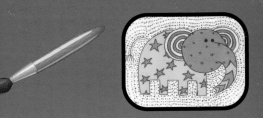

10 To finish the piece, clean your brush and cover it with orange paint. With the tip of the brush, paint some dots in any spaces left over. Last of all, paint a big orange border around the edges of the paper. Nice one!

how to paint a monkey scene using gouache

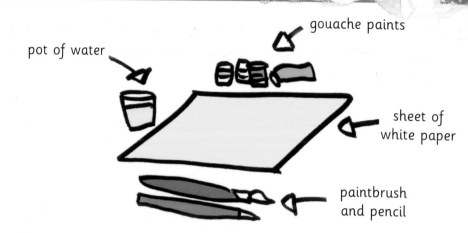

pot of water

gouache paints

sheet of white paper

paintbrush and pencil

you will need:

Earlier (page 22) we looked at how to draw monkeys. Now we'll try painting them! I've used gouache paints as they give a nice flat colour, but any type of paint will do.

❶ Get a piece of paper and draw out your monkey jungle scene. Fill the page with lots of leaves, vines and branches.

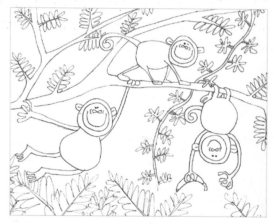

❷ Paint the background with a light green, taking care not to smudge over any line

❸ Get a light brown and paint in the branches.

❹ With the leaves and vines, choose what shades of green and brown you want.

5 When you're happy with the background and leaves, start on the monkeys. I coloured their bodies with a thick dark brown. It's a good colour to choose because it makes them stand out from the background.

6 For the faces you want to use a flesh-coloured paint. If you can't find one, mix some white with some brown and a tiny bit of pink.

7 When the faces are dry, get a very small paintbrush and carefully paint in the mouth, nose and eyes on each of the monkeys. If you don't have a fine enough paintbrush, a pen or colouring pencil will do. Aren't they fab?

how to paint a sheep scene wit cotton wool buds!

you will need:

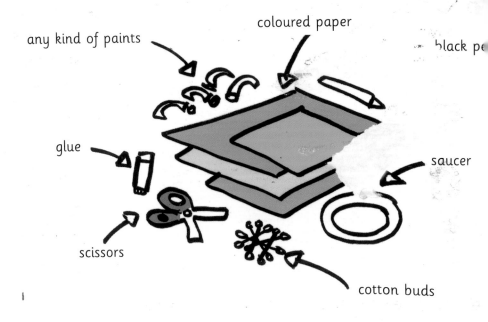

any kind of paints

coloured paper

black pe

glue

saucer

scissors

cotton buds

A useful thing to remember about paint is that you don't always have to use a paintbrush to create a picture. Today we are going to use cotton buds instead!

❶ First of all we need to make a collage background. Start by taking your scissors, cutting out a yellow circle, and sticking it down on a sheet of blue paper.

❷ Get some green paper and cut out a little hill. Use your glue to stick it onto the bottom right-hand corner of your page so that it just overlaps your sun.